Oxford SPeLLING

Dr Tessa Daffern

STUDENT
BOOK
2

Name: _____

Class: _____

OXFORD
UNIVERSITY PRESS
AUSTRALIA & NEW ZEALAND

OXFORD
UNIVERSITY PRESS

Oxford University Press is a department of the University of Oxford.
It furthers the University's objective of excellence in research,
scholarship, and education by publishing worldwide. Oxford is a registered
trademark of Oxford University Press in the UK and in certain other
countries.

Published in Australia by
Oxford University Press
Level 8, 737 Bourke Street, Docklands, Victoria 3008, Australia.

ISBN 9780190326104

Reproduction and communication for educational purposes
The Australian *Copyright Act 1968* (the Act) allows educational institutions that
are covered by remuneration arrangements with Copyright Agency to reproduce
and communicate certain material for educational purposes. For more information,
see copyright.com.au.

Edited by Barbara Delissen
Cover illustration by Lisa Hunt
Illustrated by Becky Davies
Typeset by Integra Software Services Pvt. Ltd., Pondicherry, India
Proofread by Anita Mullick
Printed in China by Leo Paper Products Ltd

Acknowledgements
The author and the publisher wish to thank the following copyright holders for reproduction of their material.

Edwardo the Horriblest Boy by John Burningham, Random House Children's Publishers UK; *Things That Are Most in the
World* by Judi Barrett, illustrated by John Nickle, Atheneum Books for Young Readers, Simon and Schuster, 2001;
The Welcome Stranger by Holly Harper, Oxford Reading for Comprehension, Oxford University Press 2019.

The 'Bringing it together' activities provided online are adapted with permission from Daffern, T. (2018). *The
components of spelling: Instruction and assessment for the linguistic inquirer.* Literacy Education Solutions Pty Limited.

Every effort has been made to trace the original source of copyright material contained in this book. The
publisher will be pleased to hear from copyright holders to rectify any errors or omissions.

WELCOME TO OXFORD SPELLING

Welcome to *Oxford Spelling* **Student Book 2**! This book contains 28 units that you will use across the year, and that will help you gain new spelling knowledge and skills.

You will notice that each unit is divided into three sections:

- **Phonology (green section)**
- Orthography (blue section)
- **Morphology (purple section).**

This has been done to guide you in the types of thinking you might use to answer the questions in each section.

Tip

- In the phonology sections, think about the sounds you can hear in words.
- In the orthography sections, think about the letter patterns that you know.
- In the morphology sections, think about the meaning of base words, prefixes and suffixes.

At the end of each unit, your teacher will work with you on a 'Bringing it together' activity. This is a chance to bring together all the things you are learning about spelling and apply them to new words!

Your teacher, along with the *Oxford Spelling* superheroes, will be giving you lots of helpful information as you work through this book. Look out for the tips in each unit for handy hints on how to answer questions.

Enjoy *Oxford Spelling*, and meet the two superheroes who will help you become super spellers – Icy Ida and Hydro Harry!

Phonology

> A medial phoneme is the middle sound in a word. A medial vowel is when the medial phoneme in a word is a vowel. The medial phoneme in the word 'sat' is **/a/**.
>
> **Tip**
>
> | s | **a** | t |
> |---|---|---|
> | 1 | 2 | 3 |

1 Say each word. Listen for the medial short vowel phoneme in each word. Circle the letter that stands for the short vowel phoneme in each word.

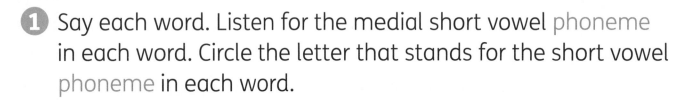

dad   king   jump   let   man

pet   stop   pink   lost   sun

2 Look in a book you are reading. Find some words that **start** with a short vowel phoneme. Read the words out loud to help you. Write some of the words in the correct boxes.

Short /a/ as in 'ant'	Short /e/ as in 'egg'	Short /i/ as in 'it'	Short /o/ as in 'on'	Short /u/ as in 'up'

A syllable has a vowel phoneme and it feels like a beat.

The Welcome Stranger
by Holly Harper

One weekend, Matilda and her family went camping near a town called Moliagul in Victoria.

3 Write the number of syllables in each word.

One	weekend	Matilda	and	her
family	went	camping	near	a
town	called	Moliagul	in	Victoria

1 Say and write each word twice. Circle the letter in each word that stands for the short vowel phoneme.

look → say → cover → write → check

man		
land		
end		
pet		
bit		
pink		
stop		
lost		
sun		
jump		

Homophones are words that sound the same but look different and have a different meaning.

Tip

red/read
they're/their

1 Read the sentences. Circle the homophones in each sentence.

   a   The girl read a book with a red cover.

   b   They're wearing their school uniforms.

2 Write your own sentences using these homophones.

red	
read	

3 Look for homophones in a book you are reading. Write two sentences from your book that have a homophone.

Homophones	Sentences

Now try this unit's 'Bringing it together' activity, which your teacher will give you.

The letter **y** can stand for a vowel phoneme or a consonant phoneme. The **y** in 'yes' stands for a consonant phoneme. The **y** in 'sky' stands for a vowel phoneme.

1 Say each word. Listen for the sound that the letter **y** stands for in each word. Circle the word if the **y** stands for a consonant phoneme. Draw a line under the word if the **y** stands for a vowel phoneme.

| year | very | fairy | yes | story | you | pretty | my |

| yellow | yogurt | lucky | young | yacht | city |

2 Read out loud from a book you are reading. Write a word from your book with one syllable, a word with two syllables and a word with three syllables. Then count the phonemes in each word.

	The word is …	How many phonemes?
One-syllable word		
Two-syllable word		
Three-syllable word		

1 Read each word. Circle the words with a letter **y** that stands for a consonant sound. Then say and write each word three times.

story			
very			
any			
fairy			
year			
footy			

2 Write these words in alphabetical order.

many	story	lucky	city	fairy

pretty	footy	hungry	year	very

1 _____   2 _____

3 _____   4 _____

5 _____   6 _____

7 _____   8 _____

9 _____   10 _____

1 What is a homophone?

_____

_____

2 Use a dictionary to search for each homophone. Write your definitions in the boxes.

knight	
night	

3 Write the missing homophones to complete the sentence.

read	red	knight	night

One dark and rainy _____ , I took out

a big _____ storybook and _____

about a brave _____.

Now try this unit's 'Bringing it together' activity, which your teacher will give you.

UNIT 3

1 Say each word. Listen for the **long** or **short /a/** phoneme in each word.

snake

rabbit

piano

train

candle

apple

flag

table

rainbow

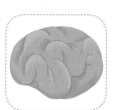
brain

Write each word in the correct box.

Short /a/ phoneme	**Long /a/** phoneme

OXFORD UNIVERSITY PRESS

2 Look for some **short /a/** vowel phonemes and **long /a/** vowel phonemes in a book you are reading. Read the words out loud to help you. Write some of the words in the boxes.

Short /a/ phoneme	Long /a/ phoneme

1 Write each word twice.

OXFORD WORDLIST

look ·····▸ say ·····▸ cover ·····▸ write ····▸ check

place		
say		
name		
train		
same		

OXFORD UNIVERSITY PRESS

Tip

Compound words are made when two words are joined together to make a new word. 'Weekend' is a compound word. This word is made by joining the two smaller words 'week' and 'end'.

1 Join the pairs of words together to write compound words.

Word + Word		Compound word
rain	bow	
break	fast	

2 Write your own sentence for each word in the boxes.

rain	
bow	
rainbow	
break	
fast	
breakfast	

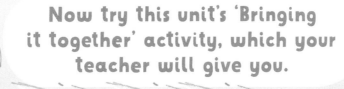

Now try this unit's 'Bringing it together' activity, which your teacher will give you.

UNIT 4

1 Say each word. Listen for the vowel phoneme in each word. Draw a line under the words with a **short /e/** phoneme. Circle the words with a **long /e/** phoneme.

| leaf | egg | cheese | nest |

| bee | pen | key | ten |

2 Read out loud from a book you are reading. Write some words from your book with a **long /e/** vowel phoneme. Then write some words from your book with a **short /e/** vowel phoneme.

Long /e/ phoneme	Short /e/ phoneme

OXFORD UNIVERSITY PRESS

1 Complete the word search.

f	t	t	r	b	e	a	c	h	f	y	l	c	f	w
v	a	e	l	f	b	e	e	n	d	d	v	e	w	r
h	t	e	a	c	h	e	r	d	o	y	t	r	e	e
p	f	c	b	a	m	t	a	d	q	f	a	u	x	e
d	u	h	o	x	z	o	a	a	m	t	e	a	m	u
x	j	g	r	e	e	n	d	y	d	k	h	s	u	c
r	e	d	q	t	r	q	t	o	c	r	e	e	f	r
c	a	i	v	l	r	e	a	c	h	d	t	w	o	e
j	s	n	i	r	v	m	w	r	e	a	d	z	c	e
c	y	t	c	w	s	o	k	r	g	v	d	l	v	k

green	creek
tree	reef
teacher	been
read	reach
team	easy
beach	

2 Write each word twice.

 look → say → cover → write → check

green		
tree		
teacher		
read		
team		

Write two more words with a **long /e/** phoneme that you would like to learn. Write each word twice.

_____   _____

_____   _____

3 Read each word. Look at the letter pattern that spells the **long /e/** vowel phoneme. Write each different letter pattern in the boxes. Then write each word in the correct box. One is done for you.

bee   be   team   deep   dream

equal   beast   queen   she

Letter pattern: **ee**	Letter pattern: _____	Letter pattern: _____
bee		

1 Join the pair of words together to write a compound word.

Word	+	Word	Compound word
sleep		over	

OXFORD UNIVERSITY PRESS

2 Write your own sentence for each word in the boxes.

sleep	
over	
sleepover	

3 Write the missing word in each sentence. Use a dictionary if you are not sure which homophone to write.

| sea | see | knead | need |

a I _____ to wash my hands.

b To make fresh bread, I _____ the dough and then bake it.

c We can _____ clouds in the sky.

d There are many different fish in the _____.

4 Write your own sentences using these homophones.

| need | |
| see | |

Now try this unit's 'Bringing it together' activity, which your teacher will give you.

1 Say each word. Listen for the **long** or **short /o/** phoneme in each word. Write each word in the correct box.

| boat | octopus | nose | frog | rose | clock |

| toes | window | socks | smoke | bottle | spots |

Short /o/ phoneme	**Long /o/** phoneme

2 Say the words at the top of the next page. Circle the words with a **long /o/** vowel phoneme. Draw a line under the words with a **long /a/** vowel phoneme.

OXFORD UNIVERSITY PRESS

hope	brave	play	go	over
train	show	road	place	amaze

1 Write each word twice.

look ▸ say ▸ cover ▸ write ▸ check

go		
hope		
show		

Write two more words with the **long /o/** phoneme that you would like to learn.

_____   _____

Tip

A split digraph is when two letters work together to stand for one long vowel phoneme, but they are split by a consonant. Examples are the **a** and the **e** in 'make', or the **o** and the **e** in 'rope'.

2 Read each word. Look at the letter pattern that spells the **long /o/** phoneme. Circle the letter pattern that spells the **long /o/** phoneme.

most	woke	flow	boat

3 Read the sentences. Circle the spelling mistake in each sentence. Then write the correct spelling of each circled word.

Sentences with a spelling mistake	Correct words
They play outside moast of the time.	
I enjoy staying hoam on rainy days.	
She washed her hands with sope.	

> **Tip**
>
> A base word is a simple word. It is the smallest part of a word that is also a word on its own. 'Go' is a base word.
>
> A suffix is a group of letters that go at the end of a word to make a new word. An example of a suffix is **-ing**. It can go at the end of the word 'go'. This makes the new word 'going'.

1 Read each spelling rule. Use the rule and base word to help you complete the sentence. Then use the word provided to write your own sentence using the rule.

> If the base word **ends with a short** vowel **and a** consonant, **double the last letter and add the** suffix *-ing*.   **spit | spitting**

spit	The dragon is _____ out flames.
hop	

OXFORD UNIVERSITY PRESS

If the base word ends with a consonant blend, digraph or trigraph, just add the suffix -ing.   watch | watching

watch	We are _____ the shadows.
catch	

If the base word has a medial vowel digraph, just add the suffix -ing.   peer | peering

peer	We are _____ at starfish.
sleep	

If the base word ends in y, or a vowel digraph or trigraph, just add the suffix -ing.   glitter | glittering

glitter	The treasure in the chest is _____.
show	

If the base word ends in the letter e, usually drop the e then add the suffix -ing.   sparkle | sparkling

sparkle	The sea is _____ in the sun.
cycle	

Now try this unit's 'Bringing it together' activity, which your teacher will give you.

UNIT 6

1 Say each word. Listen for the **long** or **short /oo/** vowel phonemes in each word. Write four words in each box.

should	took	balloon	stood	good

rude	could	noodles	drew	June

Short /oo/ phoneme as in 'book'	**Long /oo/** phoneme as in 'boot'

1 Write each word twice.

look ➞ say ➞ cover ➞ write ➞ check

blue		
soon		
kangaroo		
fruit		

OXFORD UNIVERSITY PRESS

Write two more words with a **long /oo/** phoneme that you would like to learn. Write each word twice.

_____

_____

_____

_____

2. Read each word. Look at the letter pattern that spells the **long /oo/** phoneme. Write each word in the correct box.

| blue | kangaroo | fruit | true | threw | balloon |

| knew | juice | suit | flew | bloom | clue |

oo	
ew	
ue	
ui	

Remember to use an upper-case letter for the first letter of a sentence.

1 Use the base word to help you to write the missing word in each sentence. Remember to add the suffix **-ing** to the word.

Get Moving!
by Melanie Guile

move	_____ your body is called physical activity.
walk	_____ quickly is good.
run	_____ is even better!
thump	If your heart is _____ and you are puffed, it means you are active.
ride	_____ a bicycle to a friend's house is good exercise.
play	_____ outside makes you fit.

Now try this unit's 'Bringing it together' activity, which your teacher will give you.

OXFORD UNIVERSITY PRESS

UNIT 7

1 Say each word. Listen for the **long** or **short /i/** phoneme in each word. Write each word in the correct box.

| flies | ring | bike | lips | nine | swim |

Short /i/ phoneme	**Long /i/** phoneme

2 Say each word. Circle the words with a **long /i/** phoneme. Draw a line under the words with a **long /e/** phoneme.

| beach | feed | fright | slide |

| high | team | green | find |

| teach | bite |

1 Read each word. Look at the letter pattern that spells the **long /i/** phoneme. Write each word in the correct box.

fly	time	white	why	bike	might
tie	try	lie	high	pie	bright

i–e

ie

igh

y

2 Write each word twice.

OXFORD ★ WORDLIST   look ⟶ say ⟶ cover ⟶ write ⟶ check

fly		
white		
bike		
excited		
might		

1 Write the missing word in each sentence. Use a dictionary if you are not sure which homophone to write.

| four | for | write | right |

Dictionary

a I ate _____ pieces of fruit today.

b The opposite of wrong is _____ .

c We can use pens to _____ on the paper.

d They baked a cake _____ my birthday.

2 Write your own sentences using these homophones.

four	
right	

Now try this unit's 'Bringing it together' activity, which your teacher will give you.

UNIT 8

Phonology

1 Look for some short vowel phonemes in a book you are reading. Read out loud to help you. Write a word in each box.

Short /a/		
Short /e/		
Short /i/		
Short /o/		
Short /u/		

2 Read the sentences. Circle the spelling mistake in each sentence. Then write the correct spelling for each circled word.

A lady and a mon went to the park.	
I have two pat dogs.	
The colour of the flower is penk.	
The san in the sky heats up the day.	
The opposite of cold is het.	

3 Write the number of syllables in each word.

world	people	continent	land	Antarctica	permanent	country	Tanzania

OXFORD UNIVERSITY PRESS

1 Complete the word search.

c	h	i	p	s	t	h	n	k	i
z	x	n	q	k	v	j	q	i	o
c	s	d	e	n	d	u	u	n	f
b	o	j	u	m	p	y	j	g	r
o	q	t	i	f	w	h	o	t	o
x	s	t	o	p	i	m	c	c	g
q	d	m	s	l	n	p	i	n	k
r	a	l	j	i	l	b	b	j	f
q	b	g	v	p	e	b	i	t	o
y	d	a	d	s	t	t	f	m	k

dad   king
end   chips
let   frog
lips   stop
bit   hot
win   box
pink   jump

2 Write these words in alphabetical order.

pet

man

land

end

shop

let

lost

win

sun

1 _____

2 _____

3 _____

4 _____

5 _____

6 _____

7 _____

8 _____

9 _____

1 Use a dictionary to write a definition for each homophone.

bear	
bare	
hair	
hare	

2 Write the missing word in each sentence. Use a dictionary if you are not sure which homophone to write.

bear	bare	hair	hare

a I like to walk on the sand with _____ feet.

b The tortoise raced the long-eared _____.

3 Write your own sentences using these homophones.

bear	
hair	

Now try this unit's 'Bringing it together' activity, which your teacher will give you.

OXFORD UNIVERSITY PRESS

> Words have an onset and a rime.
>
> The sound that comes before the first vowel is called the onset.
> The vowel and any other sounds that follow are called the rime.
>
> In the word 'dog', **d** stands for the onset and **og** stands for the rime.

1 Write words using the onsets and rimes.

Rimes	**ell** as in 'shell'	**ill** as in 'fill'	**all** or **awl** as in 'call' or 'crawl'

f_____   b_____   t_____   c_____   s_____

w_____   y_____   ch_____   sh_____   st_____

dr_____   sm_____   gr_____   sp_____

2 Read the sentences. Use **ill**, **ell** and **all** to complete the words.

a   I found a large **sh**_____ at the beach.

b   In the city, there are a few **sm**_____ buildings and

many **t**_____ buildings.

c   I went to the doctor because I was not feeling **w**_____.

d   The water might **sp**_____ over the edge of the cup.

e   A **dr**_____ was used to fix the broken chair.

1 Complete the word search.

a	e	x	e	w	s	p	t	k	f	b	n	p	y	r
r	f	g	l	f	o	o	t	b	a	l	l	c	p	g
o	x	e	p	t	f	f	e	l	l	r	r	o	o	w
h	e	l	p	r	x	f	t	e	l	l	w	u	o	o
x	u	i	m	o	t	w	w	x	q	j	a	g	l	l
t	n	q	z	s	t	i	l	l	w	i	l	a	i	f
s	u	n	t	i	l	q	i	c	l	o	k	a	b	l
j	i	h	l	n	s	k	x	q	j	f	d	a	n	w
t	l	b	j	d	o	l	l	x	n	t	o	l	d	i
m	r	g	s	l	k	r	a	f	w	d	j	g	d	q

fell   doll
tell   told
help   wolf
still   pool
until   walk
football

2 Write these words in alphabetical order.

fell   tell   told   help   wolf

still   pool   until   walk   football

1 _____   2 _____

3 _____   4 _____

5 _____   6 _____

7 _____   8 _____

9 _____   10 _____

Tip

When the letter **a** comes before the letter **l**, it often stands for the **/aw/** sound.

OXFORD UNIVERSITY PRESS

1 Join the two words together to write a compound word.

Word + Word		Compound word
foot	ball	

2 Write your own sentence for each word in the boxes.

foot	
ball	
football	

3 Use a dictionary to search for each homophone. Write your definitions in the boxes.

wait	
weight	

4 Write the missing word in each sentence.   wait   weight

a   The _____ of the bag is less than the box.

b   Please _____ for the teacher to arrive.

Now try this unit's 'Bringing it together' activity, which your teacher will give you.

UNIT 10

1 Write words using the onsets and rimes.

Rimes	alk, aulk or ork as in 'walk', 'baulk' or 'stork'	ilk as in 'milk'	ulk as in 'bulk'

m_____   w_____   t_____   s_____

b_____   ch_____   st_____

2 Read the sentences. Use **alk**, **ilk** or **ulk** to complete the words.

   a   The blue dress is made of **s**_____.

   b   He felt sad and started to **s**_____.

   c   We wrote our names using blue **ch**_____.

1 Write each word twice.

look ⟶ say ⟶ cover ⟶ write ⟶ check

fast		
fire		
dancing		
second		
chocolate		

It can be hard to remember the spelling of some words. A mnemonic is a way to help you remember how to spell tricky words. It could be a funny saying or a rhyme. It could also be an acronym. An acronym uses the first letter of each word to spell a new word.

Here is a mnemonic for the word 'because'. Use the first letter of each word in this sentence to spell 'because'.

Big **e**lephants **c**an **a**lways **u**nderstand **s**mall **e**lephants.

2 Create your own memory trick to help you remember how to spell the word 'chocolate'.

_____

_____

_____

A verb is a happening word. It tells us what happens.

Tense is the way a word is written that shows whether something is in the past, present or future. Past tense means something happened before. We can usually tell that a verb is in the past tense from its ending.

Most verbs in past tense are spelled using the suffix **-ed**, such as 'played'. Sometimes the base verb needs to change when the suffix is added.

1 Read each spelling rule on the next two pages. Use the rule to help you complete the sentence. Then use the word provided to write your own sentence using the rule.

Morphology

> **If the base word ends with a short vowel letter and then a consonant letter, double the last letter and add the suffix -ed. Do not double the last letter if the last letter is x.**   trip | tripped

trip	I _____ over the rock.
hop	

> **If the base word ends with a consonant blend, digraph or trigraph, just add the suffix -ed.**   jump | jumped

jump	We _____ on the trampoline.
crash	

> **If the base word has a medial vowel digraph, just add the suffix -ed.**   float | floated

float	The logs _____ down the river.
reach	

> **If the base word ends in a vowel digraph or trigraph such as *ay, ow* or *igh*, usually just add the suffix -ed.**   play | played

play	We _____ games for hours.
show	

OXFORD UNIVERSITY PRESS

| sparkle | The sea _____ in the morning sun. |
| nibble | |

| hurry | We _____ to get to the bus stop. |
| tidy | |

2 Write the missing homophone in each sentence.

| dear | deer | buy | by | bye |

a   Oh _____, I spilled my milk.

b   Let's go to the shops to _____ some eggs.

c   I stood at the door, waving and saying '_____'.

d   The _____ watched us as we walked.

e   This tree was planted _____ our friend.

Now try this unit's 'Bringing it together' activity, which your teacher will give you.

Phonology

1 Write words using the onsets and rimes.

Rimes	*udge* as in 'nudge'	*idge* as in 'ridge'	*edge* as in 'hedge'

b_____   f_____   h_____

r_____   j_____   w_____

l_____   br_____   fr_____

2 Read the sentences. Use **udge**, **idge** and **edge** to complete the words.

a   We walked over the **br**_____.

b   There is a bushy **h**_____ at the front of the house.

c   The **j**_____ gave a prize to the best dancer.

Orthography

1 Write each word twice.

look ⟶ say ⟶ cover ⟶ write ⟶ check

giant		
magic		

cage		
jungle		
jump		

2 Read each word. Look at the letter pattern involving the **/j/** phoneme. Write each word in the correct box.

fridge giant cage jungle magic bridge

enjoy Japan wedge gentle image origin

j	
ge	
dge	
gi	

1 Write sentences in past tense. Read the examples to help you. Remember to follow the rules for adding the suffix **-ed**.

> **If the** base word **ends with a short** vowel **letter and then a** consonant **letter, double the last letter and add the** suffix -ed. **Do not double the last letter if the last letter is** x.

flip	I **flipped** the coin.
skip	

> **If the** base word **ends with a consonant** blend, digraph **or** trigraph, **just add the** suffix -ed.

crash	The toy cars **crashed** into each other.
rest	

> **If the** base word **has a medial vowel** digraph, **just add the** suffix -ed.

soak	He **soaked** the rice in water.
rain	

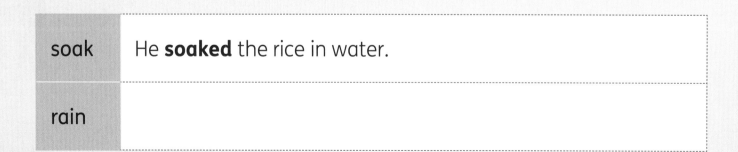

stay	I **stayed** inside when it was raining.
cheer	

cuddle	The baby **cuddled** the teddy.
paddle	

carry	I **carried** the box to the room.
study	

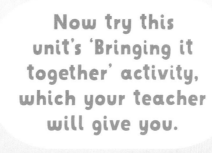

Now try this unit's 'Bringing it together' activity, which your teacher will give you.

UNIT 12

Tip

Some phonemes are voiced and some phonemes are unvoiced. An example of a voiced consonant phoneme is **/v/**. This sound is made using your voice. An example of an unvoiced consonant phoneme is **/f/**. This sound is made using your breath rather than your voice.

1. Say each word. Circle the words with an unvoiced **/f/** phoneme. Draw a line under the words with a voiced **/v/** phoneme.

| gave | fell | have | wolf | graph | never | Friday |

| alphabet | everyone | football | love | behave |

| photograph | give | dolphin | of | half | halves |

2. Say each word and count the syllables.

| photograph | love | football |

Write the words in the correct boxes. Then count the phonemes in each word.

	The word is ...	How many phonemes?
One-syllable word		
Two-syllable word		
Three-syllable word		

40

OXFORD UNIVERSITY PRESS

1 Write each word twice.

look ···▶ say ···▶ cover ···▶ write ···▶ check

give		
gave		
never		
football		
Friday		

Tip

If a word ends with a **/v/** phoneme, it usually ends with the letters **ve**.

2 Write the letters **ve** to complete the words. Say each word. Then write each word again on the lines below.

li___ ___   ha___ ___   do___ ___

_____   _____   _____

forgi___ ___   belie___ ___   oli___ ___

_____   _____   _____

3 Read each word. Look at the letter pattern that spells the **/f/** phoneme. Write each word in the correct box.

photo   off   family   enough   alphabet

cough   different   favourite

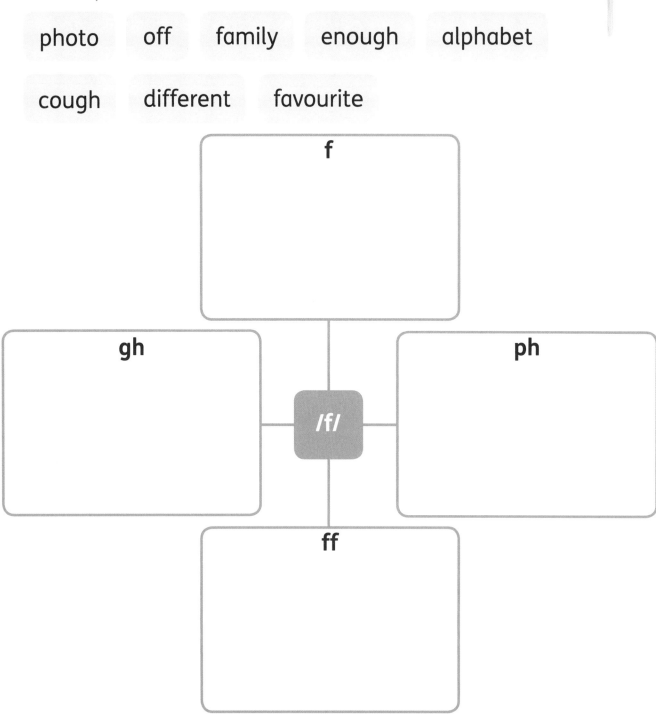

f

gh

/f/

ph

ff

Morphology

OXFORD UNIVERSITY PRESS

1 Follow the rules to write the missing plural nouns.

> If a base word ends in **s, x, z, ch** or **sh**, add the suffix **-es**.

| glass | There are four _____ of juice on the table. |

> If a base word ends in **f** or **fe**, it is usual to change the **f** or **fe** to a **v** and then add the suffix **-es**.

| shelf | The school library has many _____ . |

> If a base word ends in a vowel and the letter **o**, just add **-s**.

| zoo | There are two _____ in the city. |

> If a base word ends in a consonant and then **o**, it is usual to add the suffix **-es**.

| potato | We cut up five _____ and roasted them. |

> If a base word ends in a consonant and then **y**, change the **y** to **i** and add the suffix **-es**.

| family | The two _____ had a picnic together. |

Now try this unit's 'Bringing it together' activity, which your teacher will give you.

Phonology

Tip

Counting the syllables in a word is a spelling strategy called syllabification. You can use syllabification to help you work out how to spell a word.

1 Say each word. Count the number of syllables in each word. Write the words in the correct boxes.

| past | national | symbolic | nation | geography | symbol |

| community | land | place | protecting | significant |

| conserving | culture | town | celebration | people |

Words with one syllable	Words with two syllables	Words with three syllables	Words with four syllables

A diphthong is a kind of long vowel sound that you make by moving your mouth in two ways. An example of a diphthong is **/ow/** in the word 'cow'. So is **/oi/** in the word 'boy'.

2 Say each word. Circle the words with an **/ow/** diphthong. Draw a line under the words with an **/oi/** diphthong.

clown	toy	crowd	joy	bounce	coin

proud	boy	mouse	join	allow	point

round	moist	annoy	shower	fountain	royal

poison	tower	oyster	mountain	loyal	toilet

1 Write each word twice.

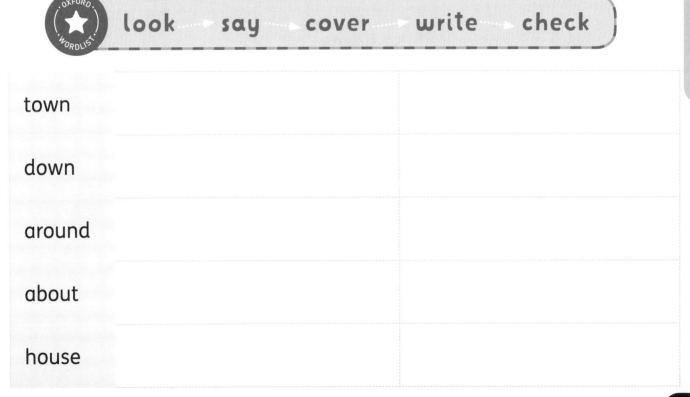

	look ⋯ say ⋯ cover ⋯ write ⋯ check	
town		
down		
around		
about		
house		

Orthography

2 Read the words. Circle the words that use the letters **ow** to spell the diphthong **/ow/**. Draw a line under the words that use **ou**.

| how | shout | brown | round | now | about | cow |

| house | down | bounce | out | shower | gown |

| town | mouse | flower | crown | found | sound |

| pounce | ground | spout | tower | frown | bound |

1 Write sentences using plural nouns (words for more than one thing). Read the rules to help you. Remember to follow the rules when adding the suffix **-s** or **-es**.

 If a base word ends with s, x, z, ch or sh, add the suffix -es.

box	We will pack all of the **boxes**.
bus	

 If a base word ends in f or fe, it is usual to change the f or fe to a v and then add the suffix -es.

leaf	In autumn, the **leaves** fall off the trees.
thief	

cockatoo	There are many **cockatoos** in the Australian bush.
didgeridoo	

volcano	There are many extinct **volcanoes** in the world.
echo	

strawberry	The fruit salad had **strawberries**, apples, bananas and cherries.
memory	

Now try this unit's 'Bringing it together' activity, which your teacher will give you.

> **Tip**
>
> Remember that some rimes can be spelled in different ways. In some words, **ought** or **aught** can stand for the same rime, as in 'bought' and 'taught'. In some words, **ite** or **ight** can stand for the same rime, as in 'kite' and 'light'.

1 Write words using the onsets and rimes. Some of the questions might have more than one correct answer.

Rimes	**aught, ought, ourt, aut, orte** or **ort**, as in 'sort' or 'caught'	**ight, ite** or **yte** as in 'light'

b_____   s_____   c_____   k_____

m_____   r_____   n_____   kn_____

t_____   l_____   f_____   th_____

sl_____   fr_____   br_____

2 Read the sentences. Use **ite, ight, ought** and **aught** to complete the words. Use a dictionary to check the spelling.

a   At the markets, we **b**_____ fresh fruit and vegetables.

b   I jumped with **fr**_____ at the sound of the thunder.

c   My older sister **t**_____ me how to tie my shoelaces.

d   They used pencils and paper to **wr**_____ a story.

1 Complete the word search.

a	e	x	c	i	t	e	d	s	m
w	h	i	t	e	a	n	a	h	x
m	w	l	i	g	h	t	w	o	l
b	e	r	d	i	t	r	b	u	t
l	s	i	e	c	u	r	x	g	b
t	u	g	t	b	g	d	t	h	o
a	u	h	c	a	u	g	h	t	u
d	x	t	n	i	g	h	t	e	g
f	t	h	o	u	g	h	t	e	h
b	y	a	i	i	m	i	g	h	t

bought
thought
caught
might
white
night
right
light
excited

2 Write these words in alphabetical order.

bought

thought

might

white

night

right

light

excited

1 _____

2 _____

3 _____

4 _____

5 _____

6 _____

7 _____

8 _____

3 Look again at the words from the last activity. Circle the words with a vowel trigraph.

The suffix **-er** can be used to change a base verb to a noun. This noun describes a person who does the action of the verb. For example, the word 'work' is a verb. A person who works is a 'worker'.

1 Read each base verb. Change each verb to a noun by adding the suffix **-er**.

work	worker
paint	
farm	
clean	
lead	

2 Follow the rules to add the suffix **-er**.

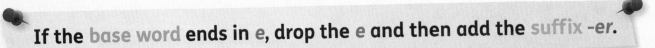

If the base word ends in e, drop the e and then add the suffix -er.

bake	baker
drive	
dance	

OXFORD UNIVERSITY PRESS

If the base verb ends with a short vowel letter and then a consonant letter, double the last letter. Then add the suffix -er.

run	runner
swim	
jog	

3 Write the missing word in each sentence. Remember to add the suffix **-er**.

a A person who sings is a _____.

b A person who builds is a _____.

c A person who bakes is a _____.

d A person who drives is a _____.

e A person who runs is a _____.

f A person who swims is a _____.

Now try this unit's 'Bringing it together' activity, which your teacher will give you.

1 A letter **r** can change how a vowel phoneme sounds. Say each word. Listen to how the letter **r** changes the vowel phoneme in each word. Sort the words.

bird	scare	dark	spare	mark	third

aware	farm	work	square	park	earth

/er/ as in 'her'	**/air/** as in 'scare'	**/ar/** as in 'dark'

2 Read out loud from a book you are reading. Write some words that have these sounds.

/er/ as in 'her'	**/air/** as in 'scare'	**/ar/** as in 'dark'

1 Write each word twice.

	look → say → cover → write → check	
monster		
garden		
bird		
work		
person		
turned		

2 Read each word. Look at the letter pattern that spells the **/er/** phoneme. Write each word in the correct box.

bird   person   third   fur   term   word   Perth

worse   worth   surf   circle   curve

Letter pattern: **er**	Letter pattern: **or**	Letter pattern: **ur**	Letter pattern: **ir**

An adjective is a word that tells us what something is like.

The suffix **-er** can be added to adjectives to compare things.

This tree is tall.   This tree is taller.

Tip

1 Read each adjective. Add the suffix **-er** to each adjective.

rough	rougher
smooth	

small	
high	

2 Follow the rules to add the suffix **-er** to each word.

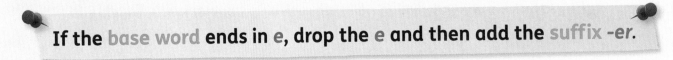

If the base word ends in e, drop the e and then add the suffix -er.

wide	wider

late	

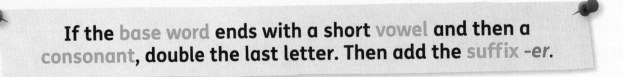

If the base word ends with a short vowel and then a consonant, double the last letter. Then add the suffix -er.

big	bigger

thin	

If the base word ends with a consonant and then *y*, change the *y* to *i* and add the suffix *-er*.

happy	happier	busy	

3 In these sentences, two things are compared. Write the missing adjective in each sentence, using the given word. Remember to add the suffix **-er**.

tall	The oak tree is _____ than the lemon tree.
hot	Yesterday was _____ than today.
silly	The first joke was _____ than the second joke.

4 Look again at the words with the suffix **-er** you wrote in the last two activities. Write a sentence using two of these words.

_____

_____

_____

Now try this unit's 'Bringing it together' activity, which your teacher will give you.

1 Say each word. Listen for an **/er/** phoneme, as in the word 'her', or an **/ear/** phoneme, as in the word 'dear'. Write each word in the correct box.

near	turn	learn	cheer	bird	work	here

/er/ as in 'her'	**/ear/** as in 'dear'

2 Say each word and count the syllables. Sort the words. Then count the phonemes.

bird	person	serving	burst

	The word is …	How many phonemes?
One-syllable words		
Two-syllable words		

OXFORD UNIVERSITY PRESS

1 Write each word twice.

look ⟶ say ⟶ cover ⟶ write ⟶ check

asked		
kids		
monkey		
kangaroo		

2 Read each word. Look at the letter pattern that spells the **/k/** phoneme. Write each word in the correct box.

cat   kangaroo   pick   crow   keep   clap

chord   cape   kite   stick   market   echidna

chicken   desk   carrot   pocket   chemist   pack

Words with **c**	Words with **k**	Words with **ck**	Words with **ch**

> **Tip**
>
> The suffix **-ful** changes a noun to an adjective. This suffix **-ful** means 'full of something'.

1 Read each base word. Add the suffix **-ful** to the end of each one. Then write the meaning of each new word. Read the example to help you.

Base word	New word	Meaning
help	helpful	full of help
hope		
colour		
cheer		
respect		
pain		

Now try this unit's 'Bringing it together' activity, which your teacher will give you.

OXFORD UNIVERSITY PRESS

1 Say each word. Listen for the **long** or **short /a/** phoneme in each word. Circle the words with a **short /a/** phoneme. Draw a line under the words with a **long /a/** phoneme.

yesterday   happy   snake   candle   place

playful   rabbit   train   apple   table

tag   handful   flag   gave

2 Look for words with **short /a/** vowel phonemes and **long /a/** vowel phonemes in a book you are reading. Read the words out loud to help you. Write some of them in the correct boxes.

Short /a/ phoneme	Long /a/ phoneme

1 Complete the word search.

t	s	a	y	s	f	t	x	s	i	k	y	o	d	l
f	e	d	s	t	a	y	b	g	z	h	z	w	f	t
a	y	m	k	h	l	o	j	c	t	r	a	i	n	j
v	d	q	y	i	a	m	a	z	e	v	r	r	f	s
a	p	c	e	s	n	e	s	g	a	v	e	u	w	n
l	e	y	e	s	t	e	r	d	a	y	t	p	w	a
w	p	l	a	c	e	s	e	u	q	t	e	j	c	k
a	c	h	p	n	a	m	e	t	a	c	i	e	a	e
y	e	d	t	o	d	k	i	r	a	i	n	z	g	s
s	v	j	w	l	d	s	a	m	e	x	q	p	e	u

place   train
gave   snake
cage   same
always   amaze
say   stay
name   yesterday
rain

2 Write each word twice.

 look ▸ say ▸ cover ▸ write ▸ check

always		
Monday		
Friday		
amazing		
yesterday		
they		

3 Think of two more words with a **long /a/** vowel phoneme. Write each word twice.

_____   _____

_____   _____

4 Look for some **long /a/** vowel phonemes in a book you are reading. Look at the letter pattern that spells the **long /a/** vowel phoneme in each word. Write each word in the correct box.

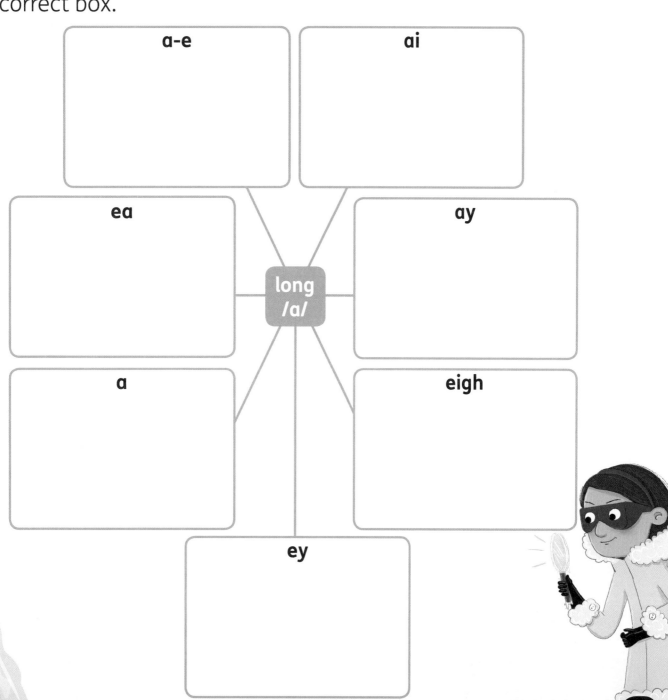

a-e

ai

ea

ay

long /a/

a

eigh

ey

5 Look at the words you found with **long /a/** phonemes. Circle the letter patterns that are not very common ways of spelling this sound.

a-e   *ai*   *ay*   *eigh*   *ey*   *a*   *ea*

Tip

Words that have the same spelling and sound but different meanings are called homonyms. 'Bat' and 'bat' are homonyms.

1 The word 'head' has two meanings. Write the missing homonyms in the sentences.

a I am wearing a hat on my _____.

b We will _____ to the park.

2 Write two definitions for these homonyms. You can use a dictionary to help you.

a head: _____

_____

b head: _____

_____

Now try this unit's 'Bringing it together' activity, which your teacher will give you.

OXFORD UNIVERSITY PRESS

UNIT 18

1 Say each word. Listen for the **long** or **short /e/** phoneme in each word. Write each word in the correct box.

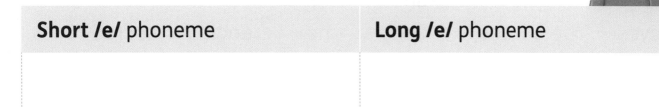

leaves   ending   please   speeding

restful   teacher   head   breakfast

Short /e/ phoneme	Long /e/ phoneme

2 Look for **short /e/** vowel phonemes and **long /e/** vowel phonemes in a book you are reading. Read the words out loud to help you. Write some in the correct box.

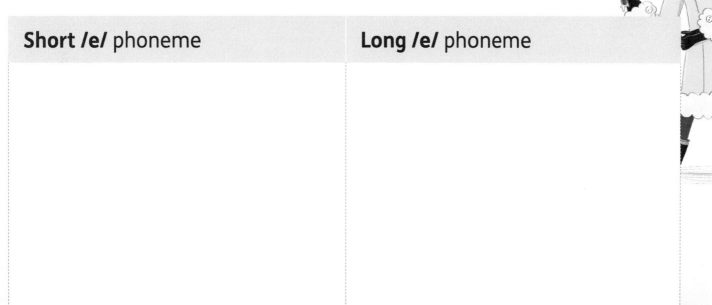

Short /e/ phoneme	Long /e/ phoneme

1 Write two words with the **long /e/** phoneme that you would like to learn. Write each word twice.

_____   _____

_____   _____

2 Read each word. Look at the letter pattern that spells the **long /e/** phoneme. Write each different letter pattern in the boxes. Then write each word in the correct box. One is done for you.

leaves   be   see   deep   he   reach   secret

dreaming   street   weak   equal   tree   cream

we   screen   beach   queen   she

Letter pattern: **ea**	Letter pattern: _____	Letter pattern: _____
leaves		

3 Write these words in alphabetical order.

OXFORD WORDLIST

look ····▸ say ····▸ cover ····▸ write ····▸ check

| green | tree | read | team | teacher |

1 _____   2 _____

3 _____   4 _____

5 _____

1 Write the missing word in each sentence. Use a dictionary if you are not sure which homophone to write.

| hear | here | bear | bare |

| hair | hare | wait | weight |

Dictionary

a I can _____ the sound of a jet.

b Please _____ here.

c I brushed the knots out of my long _____

d I like to walk with _____ feet.

Now try this unit's 'Bringing it together' activity, which your teacher will give you.

1 Say each word. Listen for the **long** or **short /o/** phoneme in each word. Write each word in the correct box.

| toes | window | socks | smoke | bottle | spots |

Short /o/ phoneme	Long /o/ phoneme

2 Look for words with **short /o/** vowel phonemes and **long /o/** vowel phonemes in a book you are reading. Read the words out loud to help you. Write some of the words in the correct boxes.

Short /o/ phoneme	Long /o/ phoneme

OXFORD UNIVERSITY PRESS

1 Write these words in alphabetical order.

go	most	hope	show
woke	home	road	rode

1 _____   2 _____

3 _____   4 _____

5 _____   6 _____

7 _____   8 _____

2 Read each word. Look at the letter pattern that spells the **long /o/** phoneme. Write each word in the correct box.

follow	hello	shallow	toad	rode	road

soap	rose	go	nose	tomato	yellow

o–e	
ow	
oa	
o	

3 Read the sentences. Circle the spelling mistake in each sentence. Then write the correct spelling of each circled word. Use a dictionary if you are not sure.

Sentences with spelling mistakes	Correct words
He woak up very early this morning.	
I hoape it will be a sunny weekend.	
A roap was tied around the log.	

1 Write compound words that start with 'some'.

Word + Word		Compound word
some	times	
	thing	
	one	

2 Use the compound words to complete the sentences.

sometimes   something   someone

a I can hear _____ singing.

b There is _____ in the box.

c It snows in Canada _____.

Now try this unit's 'Bringing it together' activity, which your teacher will give you.

UNIT 20

1 Say each word. Circle the words with a **short /o/** phoneme, as in the word 'not'. Draw a line under the words with a **short /oo/** phoneme, as in the word 'book'.

chook	hot	spot	should	took	squash

stood	good	watch	rock	would	bottle

could	wool	hopping	long

2 Read out loud from a book you are reading. Look for words with a **short /oo/** vowel phoneme, as in the word 'book'. Write three of the words in the boxes. Then write the sentence you found it in.

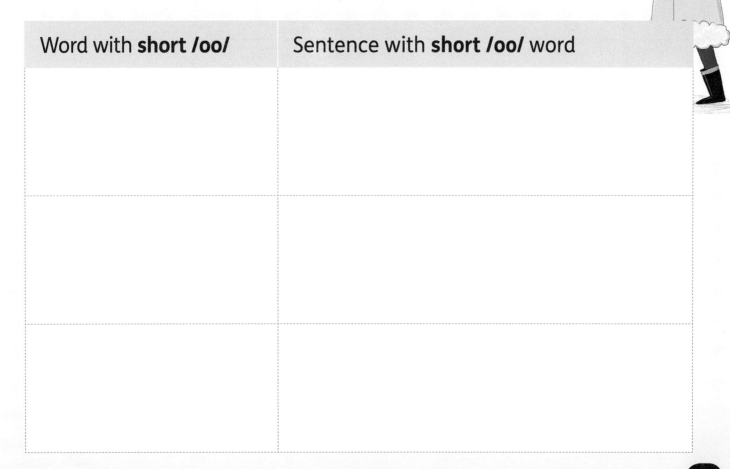

Word with **short /oo/**	Sentence with **short /oo/** word

1 Write each word twice.

look ····▸ say ····▸ cover ····▸ write ····▸ check

footy	
look	
book	
could	

2 Think of two words with a **short /oo/** phoneme, as in the word 'book', that you find tricky to spell. Write each word twice.

_____   _____

_____   _____

3 Say each word. Listen for the **short /oo/** phoneme in each word. Look at the letter pattern that spells this vowel phoneme. Write each different letter pattern in the boxes. Then circle the letter pattern in each word that stands for the **short /oo/** phoneme.

cook	should	push	look	would	pull
full	foot	stood	butcher	could	put

Letter pattern: **oo**   Letter pattern: _____   Letter pattern: _____

A contraction is two words joined together with some letters missing. An apostrophe replaces the missing letters.

For example, the words 'they' and 'are' form the contraction 'they're'. The apostrophe is where the letter **a** used to be.

Tip

1 Read each pair of words listed below in the first two columns. Circle the part of each word pair that has been replaced with an apostrophe to make the contractions.

word	word	contraction
could	not	couldn't
can	not	can't
was	not	wasn't
that	is	that's
I	will	I'll

2 Read each sentence. Rewrite each sentence but change the bold words to contractions.

a I **could not** open the door.

_____

b I **can not** see through the window.

_____

c The dog **was not** hungry.

_____

d **That is** the funniest joke ever.

_____

e **I will** go for a swim today.

_____

3 Write the missing word in each sentence. Use a dictionary to help you if you are not sure which homophone to write.

| wood | would | no | know | our | hour |

a There are _____ apples left in the fruit bowl.

b The shop will close in one _____.

c The dining table is made out of _____.

Now try this unit's 'Bringing it together' activity, which your teacher will give you.

OXFORD UNIVERSITY PRESS

1 Say each word. Listen for the **long** or **short /i/** phoneme in each word. Write each word in the correct box.

spider   bridge   five   ring   kite   stick

Short /i/ phoneme	Long /i/ phoneme

2 Say each word. Listen for the long vowel phoneme in each word. Write each word in the correct box.

beach   fright   field   green   decide   find

Long /i/ phoneme	Long /e/ phoneme

1 Write these words in alphabetical order.

(OXFORD WORDLIST)

fly	time	white	ride	life

like	excited	while

1 _____   2 _____

3 _____   4 _____

5 _____   6 _____

7 _____   8 _____

2 Read each word. Look at the letter pattern that spells the **long /i/** phoneme. Write each word in the correct box.

fly	why	bike	tie	ride	like	high

tonight	July	pie	bright	lie

Letter pattern: *ie*	Letter pattern: *i–e*	Letter pattern: *igh*	Letter pattern: *y*

OXFORD UNIVERSITY PRESS

Things That Are Most in the World

by Judi Barrett

The **silliest** thing in the world is a chicken in a frog costume.

The **hottest** thing in the world is a fire-breathing dragon eating a pepperoni pizza.

1 Read the sentences above. Look at how they use the suffix **-est**. This suffix means 'most'.

> If the base word **ends in a** consonant **and then** y**, change the** y **to** i **and add the** suffix -est.   silly | silliest

> If the base word **ends in a** vowel **and then a** consonant**, double the last letter and add the** suffix -est.   hot | hottest

2 Add the missing words to create your own sentences. Use the base word next to each sentence and combine it with the suffix **-est**.

long

The _____ thing in the world is a

_____

_____.

smelly	The _____ thing in the world is a _____ _____ .
odd	The _____ thing in the world is a _____ _____ .
high	The _____ thing in the world is a _____ _____ .
big	The _____ thing in the world is a _____ _____ .
loud	The _____ thing in the world is a _____ _____ .

Now try this unit's 'Bringing it together' activity, which your teacher will give you.

OXFORD UNIVERSITY PRESS

UNIT 22

1 Write words using the onsets and rimes.

Rimes	*ice* as in 'mice'	*ace* as in 'face'

d_____   f_____   l_____   m_____   n_____

tw_____   tr_____   br_____   gr_____   pr_____

sp_____   pl_____   r_____   sl_____

Tip

A disyllabic word is a word with two syllables.

To help you work out which syllable is accented, clap the beats in each word. Notice that an accented syllable will have a stronger clap.

2 Say each word and clap along with the syllables. Circle the words with an accented first syllable.

bottle	faster	balloon	ripple	remind	prefer
castle	away	teacher	mistake	smallest	
believe	playful	behave	before	jungle	

3 Write two words from the list in the previous activity with accented second syllables.

_____

_____

1 Write each word twice.

look ➤ say ➤ cover ➤ write ➤ check

OXFORD WORDLIST

animal		
evil		
castle		
ice		
face		

2 An unaccented syllable at the end of a word can be tricky to spell. The words below end with an unaccented syllable. Say each word. Look at the letter pattern at the end of each word. Then write each word in the correct box.

jungle   animal   evil   people   April

medal   pedal   sprinkle   pencil

Letter pattern: *le*	Letter pattern: *al*	Letter pattern: *il*

Edwardo the Horriblest Boy
by John Burningham

Edwardo became **noisier** and **noisier**.

Edwardo became **ruder** and **ruder**.

1 Look at how the sentences above follow the suffix rules.

> If the base word ends in a consonant and then *y*, change the *y* to *i* and add the suffix *-er*.

> If the base word ends in *e*, drop the *e* and then add the suffix *-er*.

2 Read each base word. Follow the rules to add the suffix **-er**.

Base word	+ suffix *-er*		Base word	+ suffix *-er*
clumsy			dirty	
noisy			nasty	
messy			rude	

3 Use the words that you have written to complete this sentence.

As the days turned into weeks and the weeks into months, Edwardo

became even _____ , _____ , _____ ,

_____ , _____ and _____ .

> Now try this unit's 'Bringing it together' activity, which your teacher will give you.

Phonology

Tip

Alliteration happens when a group of words start with the same sound. An example is **b**ig **b**lack **b**ears.

1 Look at a book you are reading. Write a part from the book that uses alliteration.

_____

_____

2 Create your own sentence with alliteration, using any of these words. You can add suffixes to some of the words if you like.

squeeze	squelch	squad	squish	squirt	squirrel

squeal	squawk	squirm	squabble	square	squid

_____

_____

3 Say each word and count the syllables. Sort the words. Then count the phonemes.

squeezing	squid	squishiest

	The word is ...	How many phonemes?
One-syllable word		
Two-syllable word		
Three-syllable word		

OXFORD UNIVERSITY PRESS

1 Say each of these two-syllable words out loud. They all end with an unaccented syllable. Notice the letter pattern at the end of each word. Write each word in the correct box.

doctor   colour   sister   tiger   horror

humour   motor   number   neighbour

Letter pattern: *or*	Letter pattern: *our*	Letter pattern: *er*

2 Write each word twice.

OXFORD WORDLIST

look ▸ say ▸ cover ▸ write ▸ check

under		
never		
spider		
paper		
together		
colour		

> Adverbs are words that tell us more about what happens. Many adverbs end with the suffix **-ly**.
>
> For example, the base word 'nice' becomes the adverb 'nicely' when the suffix **-ly** is added. They played *nicely*.

Tip

1 Add the suffix **-ly** to each base word to make an adverb that completes each sentence.

Base word	Sentence
safe	We walked across the road _____.
slow	The snake _____ slithered.

> **If the base word ends in the letter *y*, change the *y* to *i* and then add the suffix *-ly* to make an adverb.   happy | happily**

2 Use the rule to add the suffix **-ly** to each base word to make an adverb. Then write the missing adverb in each sentence.

Base word	Adverb		Base word	Adverb
busy			heavy	

a Builders _____ worked with their hammers.

b It rained _____ for days.

An adjective is a word that describes a person, place or thing. It tells us what something is like. Some adjectives end with the suffix **-y**.

Tip

If the base word ends with a vowel and then a consonant, double the last letter. Then add the suffix **-y** to make an adjective.   fun | funny

3 Use the rule to help you add the suffix **-y** to each base word to make an adjective. Then write the missing adjective in each sentence.

Base word	Adjective
yum	

Base word	Adjective
sleep	

a We ate all the _____ food.

b I saw a _____ bear at the zoo.

Now try this unit's 'Bringing it together' activity, which your teacher will give you.

Phonology

1 Write each word in the box that matches the consonant blend at its beginning.

brave	train	crow	brown	dragon

grand	drink	grow	tree	create

/br/	/dr/	/tr/	/gr/	/cr/

2 Say each word and count the syllables. Sort the words. Then write the phonemes.

dragon	trampoline	train	cradle	brave	greediest

	The word is …	How many phonemes?
One-syllable words		
Two-syllable words		
Three-syllable words		

OXFORD UNIVERSITY PRESS

1 Write each word twice.

look ⟶ say ⟶ cover ⟶ write ⟶ check

grandma		
class		
mummy		
bubbles		
happy		
lollies		

Tip

If the first syllable of a two-syllable has a short vowel letter followed by one consonant letter, it is common to double the medial consonant letter. An example is 'ra**bb**it'.

2 Write the missing consonant in the two-syllable words. One is done for you. Say each word and clap each syllable in the word.

rab**b**it   drib___le   gob___le   mam___al   gig___le   wad___le

bot___le   mid___le   bub___le   hap___y   lol___y   pil___ow

Look again at the words. Draw a line under the letter that stands for the short vowel in the first syllable of each word. For example, underline the **a** in 'rabbit': r<u>a</u>bbit.

1 Read each word. Then write the base word beside each word.

bravely		safely	
busily		sleepy	
funny		slowly	
greedy		smelly	
happily		squeaky	
heavily		yummy	
loudly			

2 Look at the words in the table from the last activity. Choose two adjectives ending in **-y**. Write them in a sentence.

_____

_____

_____

> Now try this unit's 'Bringing it together' activity, which your teacher will give you.

OXFORD UNIVERSITY PRESS

1 Write words using the onsets and rimes.

Rimes	**ay** as in 'bay', **ey** as in 'they', **eigh** as in 'weigh'	**ail** as in 'mail', **ale** as in 'pale'

b _____ d _____ f _____ h _____

m _____ p _____ r _____ s _____

t _____ w _____ wh _____ sn _____

st _____ pl _____ tr _____ spr _____

2 Read out loud from a book you are reading. Count the syllables in the words you are reading. Write some of the words in the correct boxes. Then count the phonemes in each word you have written.

	The word is ...	How many phonemes?
One-syllable word		
Two-syllable words		
Three-syllable words		

1 Write each word twice.

look ▸ say ▸ cover ▸ write ▸ check

tree	
or	
door	
morning	
forest	

1 Read the rules for adding the suffixes **-ing** and **-ed**. Use the rules to help you to write the missing words.

> If the base word **ends with a short vowel and then a consonant, double the last letter. Then add the suffix -ing or -ed.**

slip

The tide is _____ away.

The tide _____ away.

> If the base word **ends with a consonant** blend, digraph **or** trigraph, **just add the suffix -ing or -ed.**

watch

We are _____ the shadows.

We _____ the shadows.

If the **base word** has a medial vowel digraph, **just add the** suffix **-ing or -ed.**

| zoom | The boats are _____ everywhere. |
| | The boats _____ everywhere. |

If the **base word ends in *y*, or a vowel** digraph **or** trigraph **such as *ow* or *igh*, usually just add the** suffix **-ing or -ed.**

| sigh | The tiny sea snail is _____. |
| | The tiny sea snail _____. |

If the **base word ends in *e*, drop the *e* and then add -ing or -ed.**

| gaze | The sea snail is _____ at the sky. |
| | The sea snail _____ at the sky. |

2 Write compound words that start with 'every'.

a _____one   b _____thing

c _____where

3 Use the compound words you wrote above to complete the sentences.

a During the storm, _____ stayed inside.

b There are many people _____ we go.

c I ate _____ on my plate.

Now try this unit's 'Bringing it together' activity, which your teacher will give you.

Phonology

1 Write words using the onsets and rimes.

Rimes	**old** as in 'bold'	**ump** as in 'jump'

b _____ c _____ f _____ g _____

h _____ j _____ s _____ t _____

sl _____ st _____ th _____

2 Read out loud from a book you are reading. Count the syllables in the words you are reading. Write some of the words in the correct boxes. Then count the phonemes in each word you have written.

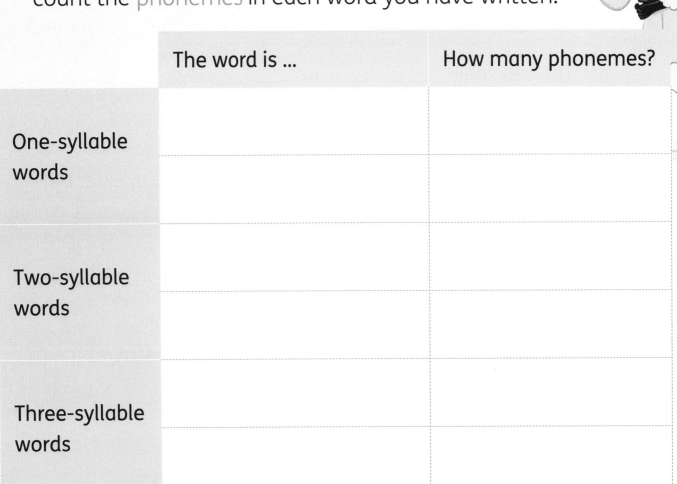

	The word is ...	How many phonemes?
One-syllable words		
Two-syllable words		
Three-syllable words		

OXFORD UNIVERSITY PRESS

1 Write each word twice.

look ···▶ say ···▶ cover ···▶ write ···▶ check

toy		
cousin		
police		
friend		

2 Read each word. Look at the letter pattern that spells the **/oi/** diphthong. Write each word in the correct box.

voice   annoy   boil   joy   destroy

choice   point   oyster

Words with **oy**	Words with **oi**

Tip

Irregular verbs do not use the suffix **-ed**. Look at how these words change to say that something happened in the past.

I *run* at lunchtime. Yesterday, I *ran* at lunchtime.

I *feel* cold now. This morning, I *felt* hot.

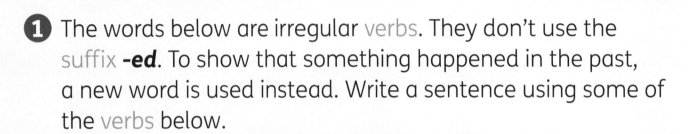

1 The words below are irregular verbs. They don't use the suffix **-ed**. To show that something happened in the past, a new word is used instead. Write a sentence using some of the verbs below.

run	take	win	sit
feel	ride	have	
tell	build	say	
fall	buy	give	
think	find	can	

Wildlife Jigsaw

_____

_____

_____

_____

_____

OXFORD UNIVERSITY PRESS

2 Read each irregular verb. Notice that these words are written in past tense. Match them up with the verbs in the table. Some are done for you.

ran   thought   fell   bought   rode   gave

felt   told   sat   won   built   took

found   could   had   said

run	ran	sit	
tell	told	buy	
feel	felt	ride	
give		have	
take		find	
fall		think	
can		build	
win		say	

Now try this unit's 'Bringing it together' activity, which your teacher will give you.

Phonology

1 Write words using the onsets and rimes.

Rimes	**oap** as in 'soap', **ope** as in 'hope'	**oat** as in 'coat', **ote** as in 'wrote'

b _____   c _____   g _____   h _____

m _____   p _____   r _____   s _____

fl _____   sl _____   thr _____

2 Read out loud from a book you are reading. Count the syllables in the words you are reading. Write some of the words in the correct boxes. Then count the phonemes in each word you have written.

	The word is ...	How many phonemes?
One-syllable words		
Two-syllable words		
Three-syllable words		

OXFORD UNIVERSITY PRESS

1 Write these words in alphabetical order.

OXFORD WORDLIST

watch   which

chicken   much

1 _____

2 _____

3 _____

4 _____

2 Read each word. Look at the letter pattern that spells the **/ch/** phoneme. Write each word in the correct box.

cheese   watch   chicken   which

much   chop   match   chess

stretch   catch

Letter pattern: **ch**	Letter pattern: **tch**

1 Write sentences that show what each homophone pair means. You can use a dictionary to help you. One is done for you.

whole	hole	I had a **whole** apple. A worm ate some of it. Now there is a **hole** in it.
week	weak	
wait	weight	
see	sea	

Now try this unit's 'Bringing it together' activity, which your teacher will give you.

UNIT 28

1 Write a sentence that uses alliteration, using any of these words. You may add suffixes to some of the words if you want to.

string	strap	stretch	strong	street	strange

stranger	straight	strawberry	stream	straw

_____

_____

_____

2 Read each word out loud and count the syllables. Write the words in the correct boxes. Then count the phonemes in each word.

strawberry	strangest	strong

	The word is ...	How many phonemes?
One-syllable word		
Two-syllable word		
Three-syllable word		

1 Write these words in alphabetical order.

look ▸ say ▸ cover ▸ write ▸ check

use

clothes

music

unicorn

half

aunty

1 _____

2 _____

3 _____

4 _____

5 _____

6 _____

Tip

A prefix is a group of letters that go at the start of a base word to make a new word. For example, the prefix **un-** with the base word 'lock' forms the word 'unlock'.

1 Read the prefixes. Notice that each prefix has a meaning of its own.

Prefix	*re-*	*un-*	*uni-*
Meaning	again	not	one

Now read each base word. Decide which prefix can be added to make a new word. Write the new words in the boxes. One is done for you. If you're not sure, use a dictionary.

do	cycle	play	afraid	turn	try

happy	clear	form	safe	corn	size

Prefix: *re-*	Prefix: *un-*	Prefix: *uni-*
redo	undo	unicycle

2 Using any of the words you just wrote, write two new words by adding a suffix as well. One is done for you.

Tip

Some suffixes that you could use are **-ed**, **-ing**, **-y** and **-ly**.

Prefix	Base word	Suffix	New word
re	do	ing	redoing

Now try this unit's 'Bringing it together' activity, which your teacher will give you.

GLOSSARY

adjective	a word that tells us what something is like *small, tall, funny*
base word	the smallest part of a word that is also a word on its own *the word 'jump' in 'jumping'*
blend	speech sounds that join together in a word ***/st/*** *is a blend in the word 'stop'*
compound word	a new word made out of two words joined together *sunshine (sun + shine), playground (play + ground)*
consonant	a speech sound made by blocking some air with your lips, teeth or tongue **/b/, /l/, /z/, /v/**
digraph	two letters standing for one phoneme **sh**, **ch**, **oo**, **ee**, **ie**
diphthong	a kind of long vowel sound that you make by moving your mouth in two ways **/oi/** *in 'boy',* **/ow/** *in 'cow'*
homophone	a word that sounds the same as another word but looks different and has a different meaning *eight, ate*
medial phoneme	the speech sound in the middle of a word. This can be a medial vowel or a medial consonant. **/o/** *is the medial phoneme in the word 'dog'*
noun	a word that is a name for something, such as a person, place, animal, thing or idea *Ali, school, cat, ball, age*

OXFORD UNIVERSITY PRESS

onset	the sounds in a syllable before the vowel
	b *stands for the onset in the word 'big'*
phoneme	the smallest speech sound you can hear in a word
	the word 'boot' has three phonemes: **/b/**, **long /oo/**, **/t/**
rime	the vowel and other speech sounds at the end of a syllable
	ig *stands for the rime in the word 'big'*
suffix	letters that go at the end of a word to make a new word
	the **-s** *in 'cats' means 'more than one cat'*
syllable	a part of a word that feels like a beat and has a vowel sound
	'weekend' has two syllables (week-end)
tense	the way a word is written that shows whether something is in the past, present or future
	'jumped' means the jumping happened in the past
trigraph	three letters standing for one phoneme
	igh *in 'might'*
unvoiced phoneme	a sound made using your breath rather than your voice
	/th/ *in 'bath'*
verb	a word for something that happens
	'play' in the sentence 'I play chess.'
voiced phoneme	a sound made using your voice
	/th/ *in 'the'*
vowel	a sound that you voice with your mouth open and not blocked by your lips, teeth or tongue
	the **short /o/** *sound in the word 'dog' is a vowel sound*

When you have finished the activities in each unit, think about how you feel about the work you have completed.

Draw a ✓ if you feel confident using these ideas on your own.

Draw a ✗ if you feel you need to learn more.

Draw a ○ if you are not sure.

Unit	Phonology	Orthography	Morphology
1			
2			
3			
4			
5			
6			
7			
8			
9			
10			
11			
12			
13			
14			
15			
16			
17			
18			
19			
20			
21			
22			
23			
24			
25			
26			
27			
28			

OXFORD UNIVERSITY PRESS